The Believers' Guide to Fighting Divorce

Loving Like Jesus to Save Your Marriage

A 7-Day Devotional for Those Battling Difficulties in Marriage

Jamal Ross

Copyright © 2022 by **Jamal Ross**

All rights reserved. No part of this publication may be reproduced, distributed, or transmitted in any form or by any means, without prior written permission.

Unless otherwise noted, all Scripture quotations are taken from the New King James Version® (NKJV). Copyright © 1982 by Thomas Nelson, Inc. Used by permission. All rights reserved.

Scripture quotations marked (ESV) are taken from The ESV® Bible (The Holy Bible, English Standard Version®) copyright © 2001 by Crossway, a publishing ministry of Good News Publishers. ESV® Text Edition: 2011. The ESV® text has been reproduced in cooperation with and by permission of Good News Publishers. Unauthorized reproduction of this publication is prohibited. Used by permission. All rights reserved.

Scripture quotations marked (NLT) are taken from the Holy Bible, New Living Translation, copyright © 1996, 2004, 2015 by Tyndale House Foundation. Used by permission of Tyndale House Publishers, Inc., Carol Stream, Illinois 60188. All rights reserved.

Renown Publishing
www.renownpublishing.com

The Believers' Guide to Fighting Divorce / Jamal Ross
ISBN-13: 978-1-952602-86-3

Contents

A Shout of Reconciliation III

Pass This Bitter Cup: The Decision to Fight 1

Before the Rooster Crows Three Times: The Abandonment 11

Crown of Thorns and a Purple Robe: The Humiliation 23

Father Forgive Them: The Opportunity to Forgive 33

If You Are the King of the Jews, Save Yourself: The Challenge to Quit
.... 43

Why Have You Forsaken Me?: The Breaking Point 53

It Is Finished: The Tables Have Turned 65

About the Author 75

About Renown Publishing 77

Notes 79

"For God so loved the world that He gave His only begotten Son, that whoever believes in Him should not perish but have everlasting life."

JOHN 3:16

INTRODUCTION

A Shout of Reconciliation

You have reached a crossroads in your marriage. Divorce is calling to you, even mocking you. As you awaken in the morning, your first thoughts may center on it. Your spouse may have said the word "divorce" for the first time. Your friends or family may have urged you to divorce. You may have received the initial paperwork today, or you may be on your way to finalize the end of your marriage in court tomorrow.

Take a step back.

You are about to make one of the most consequential decisions of your life. You need the wisdom and direction of God for this moment. If your husband or wife has spoken the words "divorce," tell them you love them. If you are thinking of calling a lawyer, put the phone down. If you have received notice of a divorce filing, take heart. If you are on your way to the courthouse to finalize a divorce, do not sign the documents. Turn around—and pray.

Seek God and you will find direction. He gives wisdom freely and generously to those who ask (James 1:5). Make sure your guard is down, your heart is open, and self-centered plans leading down a path of divorce are thrown away. You will hear from God. The discouraging whisper of "divorce" will be replaced with an encouraging shout of "reconciliation" that fills your soul.

Consider John 3:16, arguably one of the most well-known scriptures in the Bible. All the books in the world, let alone a single devotional, cannot encapsulate the infinite depths of meaning within this scripture. Yet this single verse leads us to a radical love story: the crucifixion of Jesus Christ. Despite being rejected and dishonored by His bride, God loves her so intensely that He chose to suffer. In light of His suffering, how can the bride say that she is not loved? As she understands the heights of Christ's suffering, the depths of His love, and the generosity of His kindness, the bride draws toward her husband. They reconcile, she gives her heart to Him, and they love happily ever after in a new covenant.

A godly marriage reflects Jesus' marriage to the church. You will have a better understanding of your direction through the difficulties in your marriage when you know the heart of God and the value He places on the covenant of marriage. Marriage is honorable in every way and brings God glory and joy (see Hebrews 13:4). Through marriage, God works a plan to bring about holy children, "godly offspring" (Malachi 2:15).

> *The sacrifices of reconciliation are many, but it is worth it.*

On the other hand, God hates divorce (Malachi 2:16). Nothing should separate a man and woman who are married (Mark 10:9). God will not respond to your tears if you deal with your spouse "treacherously," or unjustly (Malachi 2:13–14), by overwhelming them with divorce. Our hearts of stone have led us down a path of divorce (Matthew 19:8). There is no point of contention or confusion regarding God's feelings toward divorce: God does not want you and your spouse to be divorced. He wants you and your spouse to be reconciled just as He reconciles us to Him through Jesus Christ.

The sacrifices of reconciliation are many, but it is worth it. If you have to destroy your pride and arrogance to restore your marriage, so be it. If you have to suffer hurt to forgive, so be it. If you have to fast and pray at the altar of God, so be it. If you have to give all your time and possessions to save your marriage, so be it. Do not worry about the time, effort, and emotional suffering paid for reconciliation. God will restore your marriage to a better state than you could ever imagine. You will lose nothing; instead, you will recover all and more (see 1 Samuel 30:18–19). You will forget the pain of your past once you walk in the way of restoration (see Genesis 41:51).

By contrast, disregarding God's plan for marriage, and

divorcing your spouse, can create ripples in the pond of life that adversely affect not only you and your spouse but also your children—for generations to come.

Do you think divorce is not a health issue? Divorced men and women have a greater risk of premature death and an increased risk of heart attacks.[1][2] They are also more likely to be in poor health in general and to have diabetes.[3] Considering the burden you may place on your health with a divorce, self-interest seems to recommend you remain married!

Remember, the husband who loves his wife loves himself (Ephesians 5:28). As an analogy, someone with diabetes who suffers an infection to their foot is at risk for an amputation. They quickly agree and adhere to long courses of antibiotics, wound debridement, and physical therapy to save a limb. Your spouse is worth more than a hand, a foot, or any part of your body you consider valuable. In fact, a husband and his wife are one flesh (Genesis 2:24). When you care for your spouse, you care for yourself.

And do you think divorce is not a generational curse? Children of divorced parents are more likely to become divorced themselves.[4] They are also more likely to use alcohol and suffer with depression and anxiety.[5][6][7][8] Think about the burden you can place on your children with a divorce. One of the best decisions you can make for your children, to steer their life in a positive direction, is to remain married.

Especially for those of us who prayed for a spouse, you may feel as though you received the opposite of your requests and heartfelt desires. You kept your heart pure and your body

A Shout of Reconciliation

consecrated and entered marriage with God's direction, only to feel as though you strayed into a devastating situation. Yet, take a glimpse outside your emotions and look at the character of God. Remember, even an evil man knows how to give an excellent gift. If his child asks for bread, he doesn't give his child a stone. How much more so does God know how to give good gifts to His children (Matthew 7:9–11)!

Your marriage and your spouse are blessings and gifts from God. In this moment of struggle and distress, you cannot understand the beauty of restoration you will see one day. You cannot understand the wonderful and fulfilling person your spouse will become. But to experience these blessings, you have to stay and fight for your marriage. Stay long enough to see the promise, and your gift, come to pass. If you leave now, you will never know what your marriage would have become.

Remember, the Bible teaches us, "No one can enter a strong man's house and plunder his goods, unless he first binds the strong man" (Mark 3:27). You are this strong man. If anyone wants to destroy your marriage and impact the life of your children, they will need to trample upon you while you remain on your knees in prayer. They will need to break past the consistent confessions of restoration you express aloud with words. They will need to cross your mountains of forgiveness. They will need to bring down your towers of hope—and "hope does not disappoint" (Romans 5:5).

Stand at the door of your home. Protect the covenant. Your most effective weapon against divorce is your long-suffering as you wait patiently for God to change your situation. You deal devastating blows to the enemy as you stand in the gap for your marriage, or maybe kneel instead, with your hands lifted in expectation of restoration. If you remove yourself from your position as the protector of your family, imagine what dangerous influences may enter their lives. Just as Jesus protected us and restored us to a better covenant through His suffering, you are called to protect the covenant with your spouse, even when it is difficult.

The Bible reminds us that a husband is to love his wife as Christ loves the church (Ephesians 5:25). This devotional presents an opportunity to discover how to fight for your marriage by learning how Jesus restored us to God our Father through His suffering. As a disclaimer, we do not advocate remaining in a dangerous environment of physical abuse or tolerating cycles of infidelity. Those situations are beyond the scope of this devotional, which addresses the many cases in which violence or infidelity has not transpired but we lack a desire to compromise, forgive, and believe the best of our spouse.

As we enter each day of our devotional, we will delve into the love Jesus has for the church by examining one of seven points in time during His crucifixion. We know we are on the right path in life when we are looking more like Jesus day by day. Use the song of the day to help remind yourself of God's promises and strengthen yourself for the road ahead. You may also use this devotion in a small group and engage in discussions with those who have fought for, and recaptured, their marriage with love.

Just as Jesus has risen from the dead and restored us to a

relationship with God, your marriage will rise from the ashes and God will restore your spouse to you. The restoration of your marriage will reflect our restoration to God our Father through Jesus Christ. But you will need to suffer for a little while. Just as Jesus builds His church, build your marriage from the ground up.

Song of the Day:
"Build This Church"
by Elevation Worship
and Maverick City

> "O My Father, if it is possible, let this cup pass from me."
>
> MATTHEW 26:39

DAY ONE

Pass This Bitter Cup: The Decision to Fight

Jesus is in the garden of Gethsemane and in distress. He has brought a few disciples with Him to pray, but they could not stay awake. He is alone. Praying with great intensity, Jesus sweats drops of blood and sees the pain of the cross ahead of Him. He asks for the bitter suffering ("this cup") to be avoided, if possible. Yet, while in prayer, Jesus puts away His will and performs the will of the Father instead.

The Bible gives us a glimpse into this personal moment of Jesus wrestling with a decision. This glimpse has a purpose. There comes a time in our lives when we need to decide to do things our way or God's way. This decision involves putting aside our plans and, instead, making a commitment to travel God's path of long-suffering and endurance in faith to reach a destination that leads to restoration. You are on the right path if you look like Jesus in your suffering; you are on the right path if you are enduring. When you make a commitment to restoration, you are fighting a good fight (see 1 Timothy 6:12).

Jesus found peace in His assignment to protect the covenant between God and His people. He made a commitment to protect His bride, the church, before we accepted Him. To this end, He gave His life as an extravagant gift to protect a covenant, a marriage, that the world had violated and devalued. While we dishonored Him, Jesus saved us and reconciled us to God our Father.

As you look down the path of restoration, do not become discouraged. You have arrived at a fork in the road of your marriage, and divorce appears convenient. The path has well-defined, paved roads. The shrubbery is trimmed, and obstructions are clear. You can visualize each turn. The road feels predictable. While holding on to pride and stubbornness, you can maintain some control. You will expend some time, energy, and money, but overall, this path appears more comfortable.

The path of restoration seems less traveled. There are no hints that anyone has traveled this road recently. There are tall weeds and overgrowth. The road is unpredictable and covered with obstacles. You do not know how long you will need to travel this road, nor how much will be required of you. Yet, you know pride, stubbornness, and impatience are required as a down payment. You will have no control. You cannot visualize the twists and turns ahead. At first glance, this road seems impossible. You know suffering and toil are in your future. The longer you stare at the road of restoration, the more discouraged you become.

You will need faith for the road of restoration

Remember, with men it is impossible, "but with God all things are possible" (Matthew 19:26). Do not rely on your sight. You will need faith for the road of restoration (see 2 Corinthians 5:7). Your first step requires a commitment to more suffering and patient endurance. Of these two paths, only one leads to God's heart. The other leads to a broken marriage.

Knowing what lies ahead, your heart may become troubled. Like Jesus, you will ask God if there is another way to restore the covenant. You may ask: "Can my spouse return and exclaim, 'I'm sorry?' Do I need to forgive while I continue to be dishonored? Do I need to hope as I fall deeper into despair? Do I need to contemplate the beauty of my spouse as I remain alone? Do I need to pray for others as they curse my name?" The answer to all these questions is "yes."

Just as Jesus asked for the bitter cup of suffering to pass from Him, you may also ask for your bitter cup of rejection, abandonment, dishonor, and loneliness to pass you by. Yet, turn your back on your own plans and say, "Not my will, but Your will."

As we examine the decision to protect the covenant with

your spouse, start by asking yourself a few questions: Do you believe, in this moment of distress, that it is unnecessary to pray to God for direction or to submit yourself to His will? Do you believe it is God's intention not to defend your covenant, while others seek to destroy it? Do you believe you are suffering for the sake of suffering, or even that God is tormenting you? Each of those conclusions is false and an impossibility!

Decide today to give your obedience as an extravagant gift to God as you to fight to renew the covenant with your spouse. "Count it all joy" and a privilege to suffer like Jesus as you understand His love for us by demonstrating love for your spouse through long-suffering (James 1:2–3). Keep your eyes on the promise of restoration as you suffer and endure, "lest you become weary and discouraged in your souls" (Hebrews 12:3). The beauty of a restored marriage will be beyond your imagination.

Just as Jesus protected and restored our covenant with God, you are the protector of the covenant with your spouse. God has not disowned and rejected your spouse; neither should you. Your spouse needs to know you will not leave their side and that you love them despite their actions. They need to know you will protect the covenant. If no one else honors your marriage, including your spouse, you will honor it. Even if you are the only one to guard your covenant, realize you are pleasing to God and a reflection of Jesus Christ.

Remember, it pleased God that Jesus was bruised (Isaiah 53:10). God wants you to be willing to suffer for your marriage! The pain will be real. The loneliness seems unbearable.

You will long for better days, but your suffering will yield great fruit. This is the love that changes the hearts of others, breaks curses, and positions you for the blessings of God.

Think of what the suffering of Jesus has accomplished. We cannot measure its true magnitude. Jesus has the keys to hell and death, and He sits at the right hand of God with all power and authority (Matthew 28:18). Because He suffered, Jesus draws all men to Him (see John 12:32).

The endgame is not for you to suffer in perpetuity, but to accomplish a purpose. By protecting the covenant, Jesus has given us a new and better covenant. In the same way, by deciding to suffer to restore your marriage, you will receive a better, more fulfilling marriage. When Jesus calls you to defend the covenant to your spouse, respond with affirmation!

Song of the Day:
"Respond"
by Travis Greene[10]

REFLECTIONS

Day One Reflections

Question: With Matthew 26:39 in mind, what is your bitter cup, such as feelings of rejection or abandonment, you have asked God to spare you from? What are some events or circumstances you wish to avoid, if possible, as you fight for your marriage?

_____
_____
_____
_____
_____
_____
_____
_____

Question: According to Isaiah 53:10, how did God feel about the suffering of Jesus Christ on the cross? Why do you believe God feels this way? With Hebrews 12:3 in mind, how can you draw strength in times of your suffering as you fight to protect the covenant to your spouse?

_____
_____
_____
_____
_____
_____
_____
_____
_____
_____
_____
_____
_____
_____
_____
_____
_____
_____

Question: Will you fight to restore your marriage, even if you have to drink the bitter cup you listed above? Why or why not? If you will fight, write a statement declaring this. Then say it aloud!

_____
_____
_____
_____
_____
_____
_____
_____
_____
_____
_____
_____
_____
_____
_____
_____
_____

Day One Notes

Immediately a rooster crowed. And Peter remembered the word of Jesus who had said to him, "Before the rooster crows, you will deny me three times." So he went out and wept bitterly.

MATTHEW 26:74

DAY TWO

Before the Rooster Crows Three Times: The Abandonment

Following Jesus' prayer in the garden of Gethsemane, Judas betrays Him to His enemies, who arrest Him and bring Him before the Sanhedrin court. False witnesses speak against Him, leading to a death sentence upon Him. They spit in His face, blindfold Him, and beat Him with their fists. Jesus is struck with the palms of their hands, mocked, and told to prophesy who hit him (Mark 14:65).

Before His prayer in the garden of Gethsemane, while at their last supper together, Jesus warns His disciples of the trouble ahead. He tells them that they will fall away and scatter. Taken aback by these words, Peter states, "Even if all were made to stumble because of You, I will never be made to stumble" (Matthew 26:33). For this bold declaration, Peter receives a distinctive prophecy: that very night, before the rooster crows, he will deny Jesus three times. In response, Peter states he would die with Jesus. Later in the evening, during Judas's betrayal of Jesus in the garden of Gethsemane, Peter pulls a sword in defense of Jesus—only to deny Him three times a short while later.

As Peter warms himself by the fire, a servant girl recognizes him. Peter denies Jesus. After a time, the servant girl sees him again. Peter continues his denial. Finally, others recognize Peter, calling him a disciple of Jesus. This time, Peter swears in his denial. A rooster crows, and Jesus looks at Peter. Remembering the word of the Lord, Peter departs, weeping bitterly (Mark 14:72; Luke 22:62). His friends having abandoned Him, Jesus suffers the cross alone.

Just as Jesus shared heartfelt moments with His disciplines, you have experienced warm moments with your spouse and grown to know them intimately. They have defended you against verbal attacks from in-laws and friends. There were vows of unwavering devotion and commitment through the difficulties of life, but now these promises of love feel empty. You are alone, and all your past and present defensiveness about the way you've conducted yourself in your marriage feels contrived.

Like Peter abandoned Jesus, your spouse may have abandoned you in dramatic fashion, with public and verbal expressions of rejection. Maybe they cast you aside at a time of illness for yourself or a loved one. Or perhaps you find yourself alone in a moment of financial collapse after losing a home or job. Like Jesus, you may find yourself abandoned by those who were closest to you, at a time when you needed them the most. But like Jesus, you must forgive and continue to love.

> *Your spouse remains useful to your marriage and essential to driving your family in the direction of God's promises.*

Do you believe Peter was insincere in his commitment? Remember, when Peter saw Jesus alive after death, he ran to Him (John 21:7). Just as Peter denied Jesus three times, Peter expressed his love thrice as well (John 21:15–17). After Peter's restoration, he suffered greatly for the name of Christ and became the bedrock of the church (see Matthew 16:18). Despite Peter's public rejection of Jesus, he remained useful and essential to the church in due time. Peter meant his promises to Jesus—and in the same way, believe your spouse was sincere in their expressions of love.

Your spouse remains useful to your marriage and essential to driving your family in the direction of God's promises. Maybe your spouse is crucial to a business you have started or a book you have written. Your spouse remains essential to caring for your children and, perhaps, for an ill loved one. In due time, when you see your spouse honor your marriage and express their love, you will forget the hurtful moments of your past and thrive in the future of a fulfilling marriage.

When the challenges of life arise, who can know how anyone will behave? We have all fallen short of God's expectations (Romans 3:23). The actions of your spouse and those around you may surprise you, but they don't surprise God, who will work everything—including this difficult moment in your marriage—for the good of those who serve His will (Romans 8:28). Despite everyone changing around Him, Jesus remained stable and steadfast in His purpose to die on the cross and restore our covenant with God our Father. Therefore, do not change because those around you have fallen away; instead, hold fast to your spouse (see Genesis 2:24). Hold fast to restoration.

In this moment, you may feel like you are living a bad dream. Maybe you feel as though you are living someone else's life. It's possible you feel disconnected from reality as the future of your marriage hangs in the balance. Trouble has piled itself upon you, and you cannot catch your breath before another blow brings you to your knees. Yet, "do not think it strange concerning the fiery trial which is to try [test] you, as though some strange thing happened to you" (1 Peter 4:12). You are in a fight to protect something that God honors and values: marriage.

You are in a fight to protect a covenant. Your suffering is great because the future of your marriage is great. You cannot imagine the beauty and fulfillment to come for your marriage in the years ahead. Especially in a time of rejection and abandonment, the promise of a fulfilling marriage may seem far off. But remember, "the promises of God in Him are Yes, and ... amen" (2 Corinthians 1:20), because God does not lie (Numbers 23:19). He will restore your marriage—just believe! Your spouse may have abandoned you, but you must continue to endure and suffer. Become a prisoner of hope (Zechariah 9:12).

As you fight for your marriage, you may desire the comfort of friends or family; but, they may not always be there. You may yearn for their encouragement, but their words may have the opposite effect. You may sink further into loneliness as friends walk away, declare positions, and take sides between you and your spouse. Yet, the manner in which you handle this difficulty is imperative. Be determined to change those around you by suffering with integrity, remaining hopeful, and looking like Jesus.

There is only one side to be on, which is the side of God. There is only one correct position, which is the position of reconciliation as Jesus receives the glory in your restored marriage. Whenever Jesus is receiving honor and glory in your marriage, you know you are on the right path.

Do not become disheartened, but be strong and courageous (1 Corinthians 16:13). Take heart in your knowledge that the rejection and denial you are suffering will not be in vain. Be determined to endure the pain of rejection for a moment to see the promise of restoration for a lifetime. For after you have suffered a little while, God will restore, support, and strengthen you; He will "perfect, establish, strengthen, and settle you" on a firm foundation (1 Peter 5:10).

Song of the Day:
"Build My Life"
by Housefires[11]

REFLECTIONS

Day Two Reflections

Question: In this moment of fighting for your marriage, have you found yourself alone? If so, how does this make you feel?

_____
_____
_____
_____
_____
_____
_____
_____
_____
_____

Question: Does the testing of your marriage feel like a strange trial, as described in 1 Peter 4:12? In this moment of your testing, what has surprised you? With 1 Peter 5:10 in mind, what will come after this suffering?

_____
_____
_____
_____
_____
_____
_____
_____
_____
_____
_____
_____
_____
_____
_____
_____
_____

Question: First Peter 5:7 tells us to cast our cares upon Jesus. Write a statement declaring you will give the emotions, hurt, and confusion you described above to God. Then say it aloud!

_____
_____
_____
_____
_____
_____
_____
_____
_____
_____
_____
_____
_____
_____
_____
_____
_____

Day Two Notes

"Then Jesus came out, wearing the crown of thorns and the purple robe."

JOHN 19:5A

DAY THREE

Crown of Thorns and a Purple Robe: The Humiliation

After Jesus endures accusations, beatings with fists of hatred, and mockery at the hands of the high priests and officials, Peter abandons Him, and His Jewish enemies hand Him over to Pontius Pilate, the Roman governor of Judaea. Pilate finds no fault in Jesus yet tries to negotiate with a crowd determined to kill Him, declaring, "I will punish him and then release him" (Luke 23:16 NIV). But nothing less than Jesus' death will satisfy the crowd, and finally Pilate relents.

Jesus is then "flogged with a lead-tipped whip" (John 19:1 NLT). The entire garrison of six hundred Roman soldiers gathers around Jesus and strips Him. They place a purple robe on His bloodied body. A twisted crown of thorns pierces His head. They position a reed in His right hand, "and they bowed the knee before Him and mocked Him saying 'Hail, King of the Jews!' Then they spat on Him, and took the reed and struck Him on the head" (Matthew 27:29–30). They bring Jesus—abandoned, bleeding, and humiliated—out before the people wearing the purple robe and crown of thorns (John 19:5). Instead of showing Him honor or mercy, the crowd meets Jesus with shouts of "Crucify Him!"

The crucifixion of Jesus Christ involved not only great pain and abandonment, but also great humiliation. In contrast with images of a Holy King sitting at the right hand of God, Jesus stood before a crowd wearing a painful crown of thorns and a robe that served to mock Him. His back burned with fresh lacerations from a whip. His face bore the bruises of a merciless beating. In all this, Jesus did not defend Himself. Instead, He endured humiliation for the sake of restoration and remained committed to suffering on the cross.

In the same way, as you fight divorce, you may experience not only abandonment but humiliation as well. You will be naked before your family, friends, and church. If you attempt to conceal difficult moments that have arisen in your marriage, you may hear whispered accusations aimed your way. Other people may describe you as "trash" or a "loser"—lead-tipped words that scar your back. When you try to conceal a separation or divorce proceeding, the intricate details of these events may come to light anyway. As you stand in faith for reconciliation, vulnerable conversations you once had with your spouse may become public. Your inward bruises will be on display.

Onlookers will gossip and anticipate the demise of your marriage instead of showing you kindness.

> *Have the audacity to believe for restoration despite your humiliation.*

This humiliation seems unbearable, leaving you to feel as though you are suffering alone. Remain committed to the restoration of your marriage, anyway! Like Jesus, do not defend yourself, but continue to endure embarrassment and keep your eyes on reconciliation. Put your case in the hands of God, knowing that He always judges righteously (1 Peter 2:23). Have the audacity to believe for restoration despite your humiliation.

As you stand in faith for reconciliation, resist the temptation to absorb yourself in the pain of your current reality; instead, keep your thoughts focused on a marriage filled with happiness and honor. When Jesus appeared before the crowd and endured this great humiliation, who could have known the true magnitude of honor and glory the world and heavens would bestow upon Him?

In this moment of your own humiliation, the promises of honor and reconciliation may seem distant, if not impossible. Yet, you cannot imagine the beauty of your restored marriage, nor the honor your spouse will give you one day. There will be a significant exchange of honor for your humiliation, but you must endure. Your present suffering is nothing compared to what God will reveal in your life (Romans 8:18).

Though you have suffered, God remains in control of every situation. Through the abandonment and humiliation, you are growing. You are becoming mature—learning to love, hope, and speak faith for the impossible. As you focus your thoughts on those things that are holy, or pure, and "of a good report" (Philippians 4:8), you are learning to have the heart of God. You are discovering how to deny yourself and value what God values, believe what God has said, and see what God sees. He is strengthening you as you learn to rely on Him. When you walk into your restored marriage, you will be stronger and spiritually mature, ready for all the promises of God in your life.

Up to this point, Jesus had suffered greatly, and in our hearts, we cry out, "That is enough!" But, as we know, Jesus would suffer further. Even after the denial of Peter, the beatings and accusations, the lashes of the whip, and the humiliation, Jesus was not on the cross yet. Likewise, it would be disingenuous to say your suffering is over.

Though He was suffering brutally, and had not reached the height of His torment, Jesus determined within Himself to complete His Father's work to restore the world to Him with a new covenant. The Bible reminds us, "Because of the joy awaiting him, he endured the cross, disregarding its shame. Now he is seated in the place of honor beside God's throne. Think of all the hostility he endured from sinful people; then you won't become weary and give up" (Hebrews 12:2–3 NLT).

In the same way, set your eyes upon the coming restoration of your marriage and endure the suffering, knowing there may be more suffering to come. Be determined to endure the pain of rejection, abandonment, and humiliation for a moment to see the promise of restoration for a lifetime. You are partaking in the suffering of Jesus Christ (1 Peter 4:13). You are learning to live out the word of God in your life. And though you may feel alone, you are never alone, because Jesus is by your side. He was unashamed to be humiliated for you, and He will not withhold any good thing from you as you walk upright (Psalm 84:11).

*Song of the Day:
"Unashamed Love"
by Ten Shekel Shirt*[12]

REFLECTIONS

Day Three Reflections

Question: Have you felt humiliated in your efforts to save your marriage? Are you willing to give these hurt feelings to Jesus?

_____
_____
_____
_____
_____
_____
_____
_____
_____

Question: According to Hebrews 12:2–3, how can you withstand the humiliation you have endured up to this point?

_____
_____
_____
_____
_____
_____
_____
_____
_____
_____
_____
_____
_____
_____
_____
_____
_____
_____

Question: With Hebrews 12:2–3 in mind, what is the joy set before you? Write a detailed description of what your restored marriage would look like. Then read it aloud!

_____
_____
_____
_____
_____
_____
_____
_____
_____
_____
_____
_____
_____
_____
_____
_____

Day Three Notes

"Father, forgive them, for they do not know what they do."

LUKE 23:34

DAY FOUR

Father Forgive Them: The Opportunity to Forgive

After enduring abandonment by His disciples, accusations from one judgment hall to the next, beatings at the hands of the Jewish and Roman authorities, and humiliation before all, Jesus is led away to be crucified. Bruised and dishonored, He carries His cross to the "Place of the Skull" (John 19:17–20). Nails are driven into His hands and feet to affix Him to a wooden cross. Upon this cross, Jesus is lifted up toward the heavens, and His suffering takes a new turn. As the weight of the emotional and physical torment bears down upon Him, Jesus prays, "Father, forgive them, for they do not know what they do."

The image of Jesus forgiving from the cross reveals an important concept. Choosing to forgive while being treated unfairly is a gracious gift and pleasing to God. Likewise, your current situation provides an excellent opportunity to shower your spouse with a priceless gift: forgiveness.

> *God will not only give you great capacity to believe and love, but He will also give you the capacity to forgive*

Throughout the journey to restore your marriage, you will need faith, hope, and love as you suffer insults, rejection, and humiliation. While you remain in the will of God to fight for your marriage, your obedience to remain on the cross is paramount, but do not obey grudgingly. Instead, rejoice in your suffering, because it is producing endurance, character, and hope in you—hope that will not leave you disappointed (Romans 5:3–5.) Refuse to be offended, and endure insult patiently. For what credit should you receive when suffering only for your own wrongdoings? "But when you do good and suffer, if you take it patiently, this is commendable before God" (1 Peter 2:20).

God will not only give you great capacity to believe and love, but He will also give you the capacity to forgive. This gift of forgiveness will not occur after your spouse has apologized, but while you are suffering. Strangely, as you continue to suffer, you will discover your heart softening and being molded, becoming a reflection of Jesus Christ. You will find yourself ready to forgive the next insult or moment of rejection. Just as we drink from an endless spring of forgiveness, compassion, and grace from God our Father, you will choose to forgive your spouse for the hurt of yesterday, today, and tomorrow. You will choose to forgive "seventy times seven" in a day (Matthew 18:22).

From the cross, Jesus intercedes in prayer to the Father to forgive those who have insulted and beaten Him. Prayer to forgive is powerful, and the decision to intercede for your spouse in prayer, despite the harm they may have caused, is essential. Jesus suffered to protect a covenant for people who not only hated Him but also did not realize His significance in relation to that covenant with God. Does your spouse understand the covenantal relationship each of you has with the other? And do they fail to realize the true extent of how a divorce can affect your family?

Regardless, you can love—despite your spouse dishonoring and despising you. In fact, the Bible tells us to pray for those who "spitefully use" us (Matthew 5:44). You can love even if your spouse forces divorce upon you, remembering that "love will cover a multitude of sins" (1 Peter 4:8). Bring your spouse back to you with love and forgiveness, remembering that those who bring a sinner back from wandering "in the error of his [or her] way" will bring about the forgiveness of many sins (James 5:20).

Despite the dishonor we gave Him and the times we refused to acknowledge our wrongdoings, Jesus still loves us. There were times we had no care for our relationship with Him, so we intentionally bruised Jesus with our sin and disobedience; yet, His love has remained, unconditional and consistent. His love does not change with difficulties or circumstance, and this is how you are to love your spouse. It is difficult to love like this, but God will give you the strength and grace to love unconditionally. You will demonstrate the kind of love that makes no sense, because you are a reflection of God's love for your spouse. Jesus shows us how to love from the cross with forgiveness and intercession. Choose to reflect God's love by loving your spouse in a like manner, by forgiving and praying for them.

Forgiveness is not only a gift for your spouse; it is also a gift to you. As you forgive, fear fades and you find yourself strengthened, toppling resentment and pushing bitterness aside. Vengeful thoughts disappear, and you walk in freedom. Visions of your spouse falling into your arms enter your thoughts, and you smile from the cross. Joy enters your heart. You feel a sense of expectancy. The enemy is confused, because insults thrown in your direction have no effect. The opposition's weapons become useless, and you remain on course.

Thank God for your spouse and bless them with your words, speaking life into your marriage. It takes maturity to look past your hurt and forgive. On the path of forgiveness, you become spiritually mature, strong, and free—and this path leads ultimately to reconciliation. With heartfelt forgiveness, and a decision to endure and love despite the coming difficulties ahead, restoration is within your grasp. Ask Jesus to refresh you for the road ahead.

Song of the Day:
"Refresh Me"
by Leeland[13]

REFLECTIONS

Day Four Reflections

Question: Through your rejection, abandonment, and humiliation, what events have offended and hurt you the most? Are you willing to forgive? Are you willing to let go of this offense? Why or why not?

_____

_____

_____

_____

_____

_____

_____

_____

Question: What do you believe are some barriers to forgiveness? According to Matthew 5:44 and Matthew 18:22, should these barriers prevent you from forgiving your spouse? Why or why not?

_____
_____
_____
_____
_____
_____
_____
_____
_____
_____
_____
_____
_____
_____
_____
_____

Question: With Matthew 5:44 in mind, write a prayer for your spouse in which you forgive and intercede for the restoration of your marriage. Then say it aloud!

Day Four Notes

"If He is the King of Israel, let Him now come down from the cross, and we will believe Him."

MATTHEW 27:42B

DAY FIVE

If You Are the King of the Jews, Save Yourself: The Challenge to Quit

After forgiving and praying for those who attacked and crucified Him, Jesus continues to suffer on the cross. The dishonor and mockery continue unabated. As Jesus hangs exposed in His nakedness on the cross, the Roman soldiers gamble for His clothes. While Jesus spills the wine of His blood from a body broken to save the world, the soldiers offer sour wine to ridicule Him. Those who pass revile Him and wag their heads. The soldiers mock Him, saying, "If You are the king of the Jews, save Yourself" (Luke 23:36–37). The priest, scribes, and elders tell each other, "If He is the King of Israel, let Him now come down from the cross, and we will believe Him" (Matthew 27:42).

As Jesus hangs upon the cross, His suffering is on display for all to behold and taunt freely. Jesus, being all-powerful, could save Himself from this physical torment, exhaustion, and dishonor, but He does not. Being the eternal High Priest, Jesus could pronounce judgment on those who have crucified Him, but He does not. As the Son of God, Jesus could call "more than twelve legions of angels" to His aid, but He does not (Matthew 26:53). Instead, He remains obedient to the will of God and suffers.

In the same way, your suffering may have taken a turn for the worst. Your life hangs in the balance, as you do not know the hour in which your torment will end. Situations you thought would never happen have transpired. Your spouse may have left without notice. You may not have seen your children in months. Your in-laws have ceased all communication. Some wag their head and say, "Why do they fight for this worthless marriage?" Other exclaim, "Can't they see it's over?" Still others call you "fool" for not saving yourself. The mockers freely put down your marriage with derogatory terms. As you continue to hold your marriage in high esteem, each insult pierces your inner being.

Notwithstanding, don't be discouraged. Remember, marriage is honorable in every way (see Hebrews 13:4). God honors your marriage and will redeem it despite what others have said. He will shut the mouth of everyone who has spoken a harmful word against the covenant between you and your spouse, which He considers holy and valuable. You may want to preserve your honor, time, and resources by surrendering your marriage, but do not even consider it! The Bible reminds us, "Whoever seeks to save his life will lose it, and whoever loses his life will preserve it" (Luke 17:33). Just as Jesus was obedient to the cross and gave His life freely out of love, choose to love and suffer in obedience to God. He will not forsake you (Hebrews 13:5).

If Jesus had come down from the cross, what would it have accomplished? After all, it was the will of God for Jesus to suffer in order to save us, His bride (see John 3:16). How could we walk in freedom from sin and live in restoration to God our Father without the suffering of Jesus? So many marriages have ended because someone quit. If you choose to accept divorce, what will this accomplish? It will alter the lives of your spouse and children for generations to come. A cloud of depression and anxiety, and an inclination to give into difficulty, will hover over your family. The effects of this decision will impact your family years after you have passed away.

Think of what you can accomplish if you're willing to endure insults and humiliation to fight for your marriage. Your spouse will know you love them, and your children will have confidence. Family members will speak of your strength, commitment, and love years after you have passed away. Jesus was the answer to the sin of the world, but the crowd did not know it. Similarly, you are the answer in your situation—pulling down strongholds and erasing generational curses in your family—even if your spouse may not know it yet.

If other people give you an opportunity to concede, reject it. When you get the opportunity to relieve your suffering by letting go of the promise of restoration, turn your back and remain committed to suffer. Purpose in your heart not to quit. "Fight the good fight of faith" (1 Timothy 6:12) and "finish the race" (2 Timothy 4:7). If you could see life as it is in the heavens, you'd see a crowd of believers and angels telling you to "get up" and "believe"!

> *Refuse to give in, and resist the urge to defend yourself.*

Just as many people hated Jesus and made Him suffer for speaking and performing the will of God, strangely, some people will resent you for speaking life into your marriage. They will despise you for refusing to defend yourself as you hope for the promise of restoration. Do not give into attacks or pressure to compromise. If you have agreed to a divorce, reverse course: take back your spouse and reclaim your marriage with suffering and patient endurance.

Refuse to give in, and resist the urge to defend yourself. Stay on the cross, praying for your marriage and interceding for your spouse. Speak well of them. Live with a spirit of expectation despite what you see around you. Do not let it be said that you were close to restoration but compromised. Don't give anyone room to claim you were close to saving your marriage but quit. Continue to love, endure, and believe.

In light of your present suffering, you may not know what you are believing for, nor what a future reconciled marriage would look like. Could we imagine how a people who rejected Jesus so intensely would be reconciled to Him? Though the concept may be difficult to grasp, your spouse does not have to accept or love you in the present moment for you to fight for your marriage. Remember, "God demonstrates His own love toward us, in that while we were still sinners, Christ died for us" (Romans 5:8 NKJV). Jesus suffered and was mocked for protecting a covenant where the bride herself spat upon Him. Yet, His kindness and suffering draw us to Him. In the same way, your kindness, patient endurance, and love will draw your spouse to you.

Song of the Day:
"Draw Near"
by Bethel[14]

REFLECTIONS

Day Five Reflections

Question: Do you feel like quitting in your fight to save your marriage? If so, why? Is it the amount of time that has passed? Do you believe anything good can come out of your marriage at this point? Explain.

_____
_____
_____
_____
_____
_____
_____

Question: See 1 Timothy 6:12 and 2 Timothy 4:7. Do you believe Jesus wants you to fight for your marriage? Do you think Jesus wants you to believe in Him to restore your marriage? Why or why not?

_____
_____
_____
_____
_____
_____
_____
_____
_____
_____
_____
_____
_____
_____
_____
_____
_____
_____

Question: Joel 3:10 tells us, "Let the weak say, 'I am strong,'" and 2 Corinthians 12:9 (NLT) reminds us God's "power works best in weakness." Write a prayer in which you declare your refusal to quit. Acknowledge your weakness and believe in God's power. Then say it aloud!

_____
_____
_____
_____
_____
_____
_____
_____
_____
_____
_____
_____
_____
_____
_____

Day Five Notes

"My God, My God, why have You forsaken Me?"

MATTHEW 27:46

DAY SIX

Why Have You Forsaken Me?: The Breaking Point

Jesus has suffered and endured great physical and emotional hurt. As He hangs upon the cross exhausted, beaten, and bleeding, with the pain from the nails in His hands and feet still palpable, Jesus is mocked by the Romans soldiers, the chief priests, the scribes, and those who pass by. Even the robber on the cross reviles Him. Yet, when Jesus has the opportunity to quit, He remains on the cross with great love and long-suffering.

Hours pass, and the suffering continues. Jesus is being poured out as an offering for the world, and the weight of our sin falls upon Him. The Bible tells us, "From the sixth hour to the ninth hour there was darkness all over the land" (Matthew 27:45). Jesus cries out, "My God, my God, why have You forsaken Me?" Amidst the insults, pain and darkness, Jesus feels forsaken—but He endures, knowing He is closer than ever to His resurrection.

In that moment, Jesus felt forsaken. Similarly, you may have been on your cross for some time, experiencing great emotional pain. The fires of life test your human will, but you have remained on the cross. You're disoriented and in disbelief, and your suffering seems endless. Time exists in a vacuum. Your old life—the one filled with laughter and solemn vows of love at the altar—now appears to be only a mirage. Oh, how you long to hear the joyful voices of your spouse and children again!

Pleas for mercy go unanswered. Natural strength withers to dust. You feel numb and limp as you withstand the onslaught of betrayal and agonizing loneliness. By the end of the day, hope retreats.

Now you depend upon God's portion of faith and hope, day by day. You pray day and night—in the words of Jesus, "My God, my God, why have you abandoned me?" (Matthew 27:46 NLT). In return, you receive silence and continued suffering.

A breaking point comes when you feel even God has abandoned you and you cannot seem to hear from Him. When at the breaking point, your life feels and looks completely opposite of what God promised. At that point, you may feel as though you are not living in the promise of God. But remember, though Jesus had a promise to receive all power and authority, He received dishonor and humiliation in the moment of His crucifixion. The Father promised His Son a seat at the right hand of God, but in that moment, Jesus was experiencing excruciating torment on the cross. He was in the perfect will of God as He suffered for a bride who cared nothing for Him.

So take heart! In the natural sense, you may feel forsaken, but in the spiritual realm, you are stronger, and heaven is on your side. You are in the right place at the right time, according to the righteous will of God. Be encouraged, knowing that Jesus understands your pain. When you feel forsaken, you are close to restoration. In the silence, rely more on the word of God. Let it fill your heart with expectation. Close your eyes, dream, smile, and focus on His promises, even though you cannot hear His voice. Remember what He told you. Even now, focus on whatever is good, holy, and true (see Philippians 4:8).

While on the cross, Jesus preserved our relationship with God. He took our covenant in His hands, hid it in His bosom, and protected it with His body. They mocked Jesus for protecting something that appeared worthless, a covenant where the bride dishonored the groom and cast Him away. Contrary to how you feel, you are in the safest place in the will of God. When we remain in that place of obedience, He protects us and guides our path.

You are in a safe place in your suffering, and you are not alone: God is close to the broken-hearted (Psalm 34:18). He has brought you into this battle not to be defeated, but to show His name is strong. God will get the glory out of this battle to save your marriage. Everyone will know that the name of Jesus "is a strong tower" (see Proverbs 18:10) when you stand firm and fight without defenses of your own—only love and hope in your heart and the name of Jesus in your hands. Then He will claim the victory! God did not bring you to the promise to lose and have shame, but to give you victory through His name.

> *You fight with forgiveness, a spirit of expectation, and belief in God's word.*

"The kingdom of heaven suffers violence, and [those who are] violent take it by force" (Matthew 11:12). The love Jesus displayed was forceful. Your marriage is part of the kingdom of God. Family members, lawyers, and your spouse may seek to destroy your marriage by force. In this battle, you may ask: "How do I fight against such a brazen attack?" It is certainly not by compromising and giving into divorce. Nor is it by joining the opposition and destroying your marriage yourself. It is through love, faith, and hope, the powerful gifts of God, that we fight. In this moment, remember to be strong and courageous (1 Corinthians 16:13).

How do you fight? You fight with forgiveness, a spirit of expectation, and belief in God's word. Remember, "the weapons of our warfare are not carnal but mighty in God for pulling down strongholds" (2 Corinthians 10:4). You are fighting a major battle for your family, with a seismic impact on generations to come. The opposition may seem overwhelming, but God is on your side as you contend for His kingdom.

In the moment, it makes little sense to stay on the cross suffering for a future you cannot see. When you're at the height of your pain, it is difficult to connect the dots that lead to the restoration of a marriage. There is no visible path. In the climax of your suffering, loneliness, and despair, you may question the path of marriage you have taken. You may ask yourself: "Does God want me to suffer?" Or, "Did God really say to marry my spouse?" Do you think it is a small thing to make a covenant before God, Jesus, the angels, your spouse, and their family, only to break it? It is better not to make a covenant than to make a covenant and break it (Ecclesiastes 5:4–5).

Remember how you prayed for a godly partner, stayed holy, kept yourself consecrated, and followed the word of God. With God's approval, you pursued and captured your spouse. Now you come to a storm and believe you heard wrong. Trouble and adversity come and you believe you are on the wrong path.

Do not believe these lies! You did not hear Him wrong, and regardless, you are not being punished for your past. The blood of Jesus covers all, including your past missteps. Continue to honor what God honors, value what God values, and fight for what God says belongs to you. Remember what God spoke to you before trouble arose. Recall the kindness and tenderness of your spouse. Even if your marriage seems beaten and battered, with only a frame and a weakened shell left amid collapse, it still belongs to you. It is still valuable.

Even now, God can restore your marriage beyond anything you can imagine. The dry bones can live again (Ezekiel 37:3–5). This is where your faith moves—a faith that believes despite our circumstances or what we see with our eyes. It is a divine moment to show we are the children of Abraham, the father of faith, who believed, in hope, when there was no hope (Romans 4:18). Hope in God will not disappoint (Romans 5:5). Keep your complete trust in Him to perform a miraculous reversal. At the climax of your suffering, faith and belief are at their strongest. If you could see the road ahead of you, would you need faith to believe?

Again, in the worst moments of your suffering, remember when you asked for a spouse. Especially if you sought God before marriage and earnestly prayed for a child of Zion, you know that God gave you what you asked for—and more. You cannot see it at this moment, but you asked for bread and God did not give you a stone (see Matthew 7:9). Rather, He gave you the bread of life through Jesus and an amazing spouse who will help and love you. The suffering is great, but the restoration will be greater. While the pain is intense, the joy and fulfillment will overwhelm it.

You may wonder to yourself, "How can anything good come out of this?" How can we know what the mother of Jesus was thinking as they beat Him beyond recognition? In that moment, could we have believed that anything good would come from His suffering? Yes. The restoration of a covenant. The salvation of the world. Praises sung from generation to generation. Breaking chains and generational curses. The pain of the cross was real—and the pain of suffering for your marriage is real, but endure it anyway. Do not give up now: "No one, having put his hand to the plow, and looking back, is fit for the kingdom of God" (Luke 9:62). Do not worry, because God will never leave or forsake you (Deuteronomy 31:8) God is still in control, and you are closer now to restoration than ever before.

Song of the Day:
"In Control"
by Hillsong[15]

REFLECTIONS

Day Six Reflections

Question: In the fight to save your marriage, do you feel forsaken? In what ways do you feel unheard? Even if you feel this way, do you still believe you are in the righteous will of God? How can you draw strength from Matthew 27:46 when you feel forsaken?

_____

_____

_____

_____

_____

_____

_____

_____

Question: Do you believe God has truly forsaken you? See Psalm 34:18 and Deuteronomy 31:8. In the climax of your suffering, you may feel forsaken, but what you do believe is happening in the spiritual realm? Do you believe you are getting closer to restoration? Why or why not?

_____
_____
_____
_____
_____
_____
_____
_____
_____
_____
_____
_____
_____
_____
_____

Question: With Psalm 34:18 and Deuteronomy 31:8 in mind, remember the last time you felt unheard but God answered your prayers against the odds. Now write a statement of faith that Jesus will deliver you again. Say it aloud!

_____

_____

_____

_____

_____

_____

_____

_____

_____

_____

_____

_____

_____

_____

_____

_____

Day Six Notes

"It is finished!"

JOHN 19:30

DAY SEVEN

It Is Finished: The Tables Have Turned

The mother of Jesus, His mother's sister, and Mary Magdalene are at the cross. As their eyes behold His humiliation and suffering, Jesus entrusts His mother to John, His disciple. According to the Gospel of John, "knowing that all things were now accomplished," Jesus says, "I thirst" (John 19:28). The Roman soldiers fill a sponge with sour wine, place it on hyssop, and give Jesus a drink. Jesus drinks of the bitter cup He asked to be removed while in the garden of Gethsemane.

The hyssop, which the ancient Hebrews used for sacrificial rituals and purification, is used in this sacrificial ritual to purify us—the bride of God. Like the believing Israelites who used hyssop in the first Passover to spread the blood of the sacrificial lamb over the doorposts, so that the wrath of God would pass over them, the unbelieving soldiers touch the hyssop to Jesus, our sacrificial Lamb. Taking the sin of the world and the wrath of God upon Himself, once and for all, Jesus pays our debt so that the Father would spare us like He did the Israelites at Passover. Having accomplished the Father's will, Jesus says, "It is finished."

In these last moments of Jesus on the cross, there is a lesson: your suffering will not last forever. There will come a time when "it is finished." There will come a time when the tables turn in your favor and there will be no more insults or disparaging remarks. Then, God will say, "Enough is enough." He will calm the seas (Psalm 107:29). As peace surrounds you, you will walk in the fullness of a restored marriage. The suffering of Jesus is part of a radical love story whereby the groom suffers for a bride who rejects Him, only for her to return better and with deep appreciation. In the same way, your spouse will return, and He will restore your marriage to a level of joy beyond your imagination.

From this point, the Gospels continue to tell the story of Jesus coming back to life, showing Himself to His disciples and instructing them to help others. The story of your marriage is still being written, too! Just as Jesus rose from death, your marriage will rise from the dead—and will shock many. Some people will hear the reports and refuse to believe in the restoration of your marriage after so much damaged has occurred.

Because of your hope, you will have joy beyond your wildest dreams. Then you will have a responsibility to minister to others and tell them how Jesus saved your marriage. You will help spread hope to others, and your testimony will put the naysayers to shame. The hand of God on your marriage will be undeniable. Everyone will give glory to Him as He uses your marriage to show Himself strong—and to mirror His long-suffering and enduring love on the cross. Just as Jesus has all power and authority, your marriage will have a new sense of power and authority, as God uses your story to encourage others. You will help bring God's kingdom to earth as your story helps families remain united.

A breakthrough in your marriage is on the horizon

A breakthrough in your marriage is on the horizon. The sun will rise again. In fact, it is rising in brightness even now as your marriage reaches the fullness of the day; therefore, do not be discouraged. When you are waiting in expectation for restoration, you may desire instantaneous change, but there may be a slow change instead. Even after Jesus surrendered His life, saying, "It is finished," He rose to life three days later!

Even after the tables turn in your favor and you see a suddenly positive change, do not become impatient with a desire for immediate results. Time will need to pass for further healing and growth. Your heart's longing will come to pass, but you may need to continue to wait. In this moment of waiting, continue to protect your thoughts and mind. Nothing is lost;

everything is intact. God knows how to protect that which belongs to Him. Do not take matters into your own hands in these last moments, but continue to wait patiently on the Lord. Patient waiting and long-suffering have brought you this far, so don't give up now. One day you will say, "This is our God! We trusted in him, and he saved us!" (Isaiah 25:9 NLT).

God will be clear about your next step. Do not fear; just believe (Luke 8:50). Be anxious about nothing, and continue to pray (Philippians 4:6), remembering that God knows what you need before you ask (Matthew 6:8). Take heart that though they beat Jesus beyond recognition, they did not break His bones (John 19:36). Your spouse is still precious. When you met them, they were kind, prudent, and faithful, and even now, their heart longs to reconnect with you. Their love for you is growing by the minute. God knows how to guard the sanctity of your marriage and protect the bones of His promise as you fight with hope. God is keeping your spouse clean as you wait for the day when they return.

And when that day comes, purify your spouse with your words (Ephesians 5:25–26). Bring them close with your gentleness and kindness. You have suffered for them; now, wash their feet. Prepare a meal for them. Tell your spouse they're wonderful. They belong to you, because nothing will tear apart what God has brought together (Mark 10:9).

You will have a new covenant—a new marriage built on a firm foundation. Watch your children honor you as they witness you bring your marriage back from the brink of disaster. Don't teach your children how to quit by divorcing your spouse. Instead, teach them important life lessons about love, persistence, and consistency by resembling Jesus as you fight to restore your marriage.

True restoration is to accept Jesus Christ as your Savior. How will you know the heart of God if you do not have the love of Jesus Christ living in you? If you do not know Him, accept Jesus into your heart, and He will change your life.

I am excited about your future! I am already overjoyed that your marriage is on its way to restoration. It fills my heart with gladness to know you will fight for your marriage and family like never before.

Song of the Day:
"Made a Way"
by Travis Greene[16]

REFLECTIONS

Day Seven Reflections

Question: Do you believe your suffering will last forever? Do you believe the story of your marriage will end at this low point? Why or why not?

_____

_____

_____

_____

_____

_____

_____

_____

_____

Question: In this moment in time, as you fight for your marriage, what do you need most? Do you believe God knows what you need (see Matthew 6:8)? What are you learning during this process? How are you growing?

_____
_____
_____
_____
_____
_____
_____
_____
_____
_____
_____
_____
_____
_____
_____
_____
_____
_____
_____
_____

Question: Matthew 23:11 tells that he who is great among men must serve. When you and your spouse reconcile, what acts of appreciation and service do you plan to carry out to show your love? Create a list.

Day Seven Notes

About the Author

Jamal is a board-certified physician in Internal Medicine and Pediatrics. He is also a fellow of the American College of Physicians and American Academy of Pediatrics. Jamal began his career in hospital medicine and transitioned to primary care with a focus on disease prevention. Prior to medicine, Jamal worked as an elementary school teacher and social worker. Through his mission work in Haiti and El Salvador, Jamal developed a desire to place prayer back into the practice of medicine and to remind all that God is the Great Physician.

About Renown Publishing

Renown Publishing was founded with one mission in mind: to make your great idea famous.

At Renown Publishing, we don't just publish. We work hard to pair strategy with innovative marketing techniques so that your book launch is the start of something bigger.

Learn more at RenownPublishing.com.

REFERENCES

Notes

1. Sbarra, D. A., R. W. Law, and R. M. Portley. "Divorce and Death: A Meta-analysis and Research Agenda for Clinical, Social, and Health Psychology." *Perspectives on Psychological Science* 6, no. 5 (September 2011): p. 454–474.

2. Dupre, M. E., L. K. George, G. Liu, and E. D. Peterson. "Association Between Divorce and Risks for Acute Myocardial Infarction." *Circulation: Cardiovascular Quality and Outcomes* 8, no. 3 (May 2015): p. 244–251.

3. Hughes, M. E., and L. J. Waite. "Marital Biography and Health at Midlife." *Journal of Health and Social Behavior* 50, no. 3 (September 2009): p. 344–358.

4. Glenn, N. D. and B. A. Shelton. "Pre-adult Background Variables and Divorce: A Note of Caution About Overreliance on Explained Variance." *Journal of Marriage and the Family* 45, no. 2 (1983): p. 405–410.

5. Jeynes, W. H. "The Effects of Recent Parental Divorce on Their Children's Consumption of Alcohol." *Journal of Youth and Adolescence* 30 (2001): p. 305–319.

6. Jackson, K. M, M. L. Rogers, and C. E. Sartor. "Parental Divorce and Initiation of Alcohol Use in Early Adolescence." *Psychology of Addictive Behaviors* 30, no. 4 (2016): p. 450–461. doi:10.1037/adb0000164.

7. Hoyt, Lynne A., Emory L. Cowen, JoAnne L. Pedro-Carroll, and Linda J. Alpert-Gillis (1990). "Anxiety and Depression in Young Children of Divorce." *Journal of Clinical Child Psychology* 19, no. 1 (1990): p. 26–32.

8. Wyman, Peter A., Emory L. Cowen, A. Dirk Hightower, and JoAnne L. Pedro-Carroll. "Perceived Competence, Self-Esteem, and Anxiety in Latency-Aged Children of Divorce." *Journal of Clinical Child Psychology* 14, no. 1 (1985): p. 20-26.

9. Elevation Worship, and Maverick City Music. "Build Your Church." Track 13 on *Old Church Basement*. Elevation Worship, 2021.

10. Greene, Travis. "Respond." Track 5 on *Broken Record*. RCA Inspiration, 2019.

11. Housefires. "Build My Life." Track 8 on *Housefires III*. Housefires, 2016.

12. Ten Shekel Shirt. "Unashamed Love." Track 6 on *Much*. Vertical Music, 2001.

13. Leeland. "Refresh Me." Track 2 on *Christ Be All Around Me (Live)*. Awaken Nation Music, 2014.

14. Bethel Music. "Draw Near." Track 9 on *The Loft Sessions*. Bethel Music, 2012.

15. Hillsong. "In Control." Track 8 on *Let There Be Light*. Hillsong, 2016.

16. Greene, Travis. "Made a Way." Track 5 on *The Hill*. RCA Inspiration, 2015.

www.ingramcontent.com/pod-product-compliance
Lightning Source LLC
Chambersburg PA
CBHW042131080426
42735CB00005B/147